Object States
Eric Selland

Object States

by Eric Selland

Copyright © 2018 Eric Selland

ISBN-13: 978-0-9883891-1-3

Acknowledgments: *ElevenEleven* (Winter Issue 2011), *Aligatorzine* (Belgium).

Cover Design: Wendy Glaess

Typesetting: Steve Tills

theenk Books
107 Washington Street
Palmyra, New York 14522

To order: http://theenkBooks.com

Contact: theenkbooks@twc.com

Also distributed by Small Press Distribution
1341 Seventh StreetBerkeley, CA 94710
http://www.spdbooks.org

"The story is never anything but a fragment, then another fragment."

> Maurice Blanchot

" I must complete the work of destruction."

> Roger Laporte

The border passes through the interior like an invisible door. Finally I found the book, written in another language. I know this man, I said to myself, when I saw the words for *north* and *island*.

That was another country. And we were different people. The pink lanterns lined the river, demarking a city within a city. The importance of boundaries. The hand was found in a dream. The man without a face.

I come to a bend in the road now, and the stone steps leading upward. I read carefully the strange characters inscribed on the wall. The trial itself is transformed, little by little, into the sentence.

But that was the last time. Or was it autumn, the north winds carrying away the fallen leaves as if expectations. I am looking for a word – to put upon, bring to bear, take out, or turn over.

This entrance was meant solely for you, the sign reads. The moment the historical index becomes legible. That this is an impossible task.

How to see in obscurity. Mirror arrangement; reticle bearing point. To recast the very notion of text. The poet screaming inside a fish.

The language of propositions relating to finite objects. This is the door. The table, the shoe; the metallic pedestal upon which the many indescribable objects linked to the system are temporarily placed.

How one comes to terms with space. There are figures that rise up. What emanates from the figure. Nameless things in progress. Now past all those images, what happens to the pages.

A man walking in a movie, adrift in time and space. I walk across the lawn. The wet paper adheres to the sidewalk. A close reading. The excess of the subject.

The plane from which everything would be made. Placing the mask before us. The immense lesson of its images. The nude figure's turn inward. She too is awake.

Space draws things to itself. Its surfaces, to which the sculpted forms. To carry that life through. The hidden self. Yet the relation is to become one which subsists.

I know the woman in the painting. A figure from my imagined past. Along the corridors of the body, dried flower arrangements and small collectibles are placed. I have her letter, the strange characters nearly illegible. They lie forgotten in an empty room, filled with books and reminders of forgotten pasts.

There is this moment. This image of light. The struggle with the materials.

And there is a door through the man's shadow, while beside him the dead child sleeps. It is hard to get close to the painting. There are recurrent themes. But I don't feel a part of the story.

The idea of proportion. The object, its specific weight. And how the image is dismantled in the moment of its constitution.

A fault line runs through the egg's exterior. Self as grammatical formality. The place-holder. A return to the miniature forms. Expanded consonance.

In the painting a man stands up. The fabulous bouquet of rotten fruit expands until it meets the rays of the awful sun. Everything dissolves. The failure of desire. The nonchalant appearance of the dog in the foreground. Why are the eggs colored that way?

There are in it words, nothing spoken. To recollect. With the past before you. The self and its double. Always something inaccessible. Sealed up like the mildly bitter fruit of the walnut.

We could imagine the whole world if only for a moment. A shape reduced to its abbreviation. We can remember it as a kind of code. As one steps into the fading light, there is a time a sound comes through. A window or some kind of opening. To insist, as a subject. A kind of vegetable, or that light. Substance which resists description. For a brief moment, it was possible to perceive something.

Suppose the body translates, without rotation, parallel to a principal translational axis of resistance. A text which is first revealed as erased or disfigured. To confront interpretation.

That space is in a certain sense independent. To experience more precisely the inner structure. The art – or the forbearance, of speaking together in conversation. But we are not at home here.

To disassemble the machine. Pulling the fiber through the access hole. We understand a speech act when we know the reason, or the speaker is a known quantity. The speaker is insulted or has a gravelly voice.

The table-like understanding keeps for itself the necessity. Takes this unfolding back into itself. The concrete shape, in moving.

When I was a child, everyone wore masks to the autumn festival. They became other people by wearing those masks. But there was never a mask suitable for me.

The city speaks. Language is a city.

The arch and the three-part columns consisting of a base, shaft, and capital that comprise the portal. The series of rooms lining the corridor. Winter Street where it joins with the main thoroughfare running diagonally to the city center.

The landscape reappears here. They remove their disguises. A face weathered and creased by years of imprisonment and exile. Infinite openings and closings. The folding under.

I see the shapes in the painting, but I don't know the way in. A river flows through the body, forming a geology of the unimagined.

The mask's tears are like crystal, seeing past the future. In the refracted light the letters appear, but what meanings do they come to? To open the breach in history.

The city as theater.

Figurations of the body. Internal tension of the object in the mind of God.

History scars the surface of the painting. In the hall of the wordless, we come to the absent presence of memory.

I poke out a fish's eye with my finger. In autumn I am bitten by insects. In every house a person sits, unable to meet the passion of the demon. Inside the egg a storm approaches. The candidate is a cipher. Everything changes in a moment.

The plot of potential energy as a function of displacement. Positional relationships: the slope of the table, the angle of repose.

Industry also becomes a cipher, a memory. The empty shadows hard at work in the factory, hammering out the complex shapes in metal. An event that never reaches its completed form.

Pain and hunger of the body. Parts that are erased. The map supplied the coordinates organizing space. The gateway. Sound invading the machine forest. Dismantling the egg.

I see the shadow line drawn across the horizon. I see the texture of future and past, fading into the background. Everything escapes me, even there where it appears in itself. Yet I lack a word to name it.

Deep in the mirror the shapes decompose. Through the liquid mass of melting corners, parts of a face emerge, break apart, and recombine. This is my face, removed from the system. Neither return nor disregard. Interrupting or tearing history itself apart.

There's a momentum that's required. Movement away from the center. When the switch is turned on the arm is retracted. There's not much space left. But then the light spills in.

The body's excess; its impingement on the boundaries of its confinement.

The book of disorder.

Sky unexceptional but warm and slightly discolored, craves deserts like childhood memories. Inside an ant hole a conspiracy is hatched. In another time it is time itself which presses imperceptibly on the border. A day which is merely a symptom. Things generate of themselves.

The colors are dismantled in the clouds. A protective cover over the field or outlet. The loneliness of the world.

It is night, darkness falling earlier this time of year. I find the letter K offensive, and yet I use it always. The first appearance of the young deer that autumn afternoon. The words caught in my throat.

The horror in the merely schematic. Diagramming the most inaccessible corners of the system. In folds of advanced synthetic materials the great highways and interconnects forever invisible to us. The appearance of yet another doomsday prediction is unsurprising.

The river wasn't really there. Streets largely empty, especially at night. The blind God turns his great head and becomes a horse. Becomes a stream of changing time and chaotic influence. The shock of history.

Filtering the materials. The egg's absence. Still no sound. The confusion about where I belong. I am never completely at home, but perhaps no one is. We invent ourselves in each moment.

It is possible, after all, to move backwards. The notion of limits. World visible at the surface. What the borders meant could of course be determined by the context.

The system exhausts itself in the process of its own unfolding. The autumn insects commence their nightly interlude. Then later a thick fog oozes up from the earth.

Virtually anything becomes material. The entire relationship. In which objects become visible to us.

Tossing the ashes like worn symbols, the words repeated three times. Boat and mirror, dream and bridge. Forms grown distant in the light.

Let us begin with an ending. The final unveiling of the dialectic. The two moments. The unity of opposites. The glass was empty. My eyes turned into a fish.

In the dream, the traditional dichotomies are structured on two axes: interior and exterior, East and West, but the relationships are inverted.

Adherence to a system or apparatus. The cup of tea symbolizing a form of affection. Again the subject appears on stage. Concepts based on embodiment and engendering. Where the gauge is to be inserted. The subject is at once object.

The paintings occupied the entire dimensions of the wall, while on the opposite end of the room a picture window looked out over the city, cliffs and sea just visible in the distance. To forestall or interrupt, to displace or deconstruct. Objects which function as containers. This distance is the dialectic. The abyss that the text opens.

Entire passages were painted over again and again, lending the colors a subdued luminosity. The turn toward winter. Night filled with the chatter of distant voices.

The street also was quiet, giving rise to that series of shapes. Only this suspension of the face provides an opening. The limit horizon. The mirror's surface. Space thus shattered into images.

The situation imperceptibly changes. Only this form of recognition. The light goes on. Which is to say, the level of the body, bound to symmetries and rhythms.

Leads back to the buildings, in their relationships. Light pours in from the window. The actual feel of it. What is thought of ceases to be merely thought of, something alien to the self's knowledge. Figures, relations, proportions and numbers. That all history is a history of the present.

May I go now, in the cacophony of voices, the breaking of glass. Everywhere is a stage. Tendencies entangled in the body. Object states. I am talking too much. Taking the hidden words of people speaking in unknown languages. The eternal dream. There is a third way. The green seed is inside the sun.

Citations:

Franz Kafka, *The Trial, Diaries 1910-1923*
Rainier Maria Rilke, *Rodin*
Paul Ricoeur, *On Interpretation*
Martin Heidegger, *Country Path Conversations*
Giorgio Agamben, *Nudities*
Georg Wilhelm Friedrich Hegel, *Phenomenology of Spirit*
Terayama Shūji, *The Labyrinth* and *The Dead Sea: My Theatre*
Yoshikuni Igarashi, *Bodies of Memory*
Maeda Ai, *Text and the City*
E.M. Cioran, *Drawn and Quartered*
Marjorie Perloff, *The Vienna Paradox: A Memoir*
Friedrich Nietzsche, *The Birth of Tragedy*
Fredric Jameson, *The Hegel Variations*
Tilman Osterwold & Thomas Knubben, *Emil Nolde: Unpainted Pictures*
Henri Lefebvre, *The Production of Space*

Some lines are free translations from the following works in Japanese:

Hijikata Tatsumi, *Yameru Mai-hime*
Yoshioka Minoru, *Umayahashi Nikki*
Kobayashi Toshiaki, *Shutai no Yukue*

Eric Selland has translated Modernist and contemporary Japanese poets for over thirty years, with works appearing in a variety of journals and anthologies. His latest collection of poems is *Beethoven's Dream* (Isobar Press, 2015). His other books are *The Condition of Music* (Sink Press, 2000), *Inventions* (Mindmade Books, 2007), *Still Lifes* (Hank's Original Loose Gravel Press, 2012), and *Arc Tangent* (Isobar Press, Tokyo, 2013). Eric's translation of *The Guest Cat*, a novel by Takashi Hiraide, was on the New York Times Bestseller list in February of 2014. Eric lives in Tokyo, where he makes his living translating economic reports.

www.ingramcontent.com/pod-product-compliance
Lightning Source LLC
Chambersburg PA
CBHW031429290426
44110CB00011B/581